# PREPOSTEROUS, PULSATING, PASSIONATE POEMS

## Andrew Pritchard

**Preposterous, Pulsating, Passionate Poems**

© 2024 Andrew Pritchard

The right of the author to be identified as the author of this work has been asserted in accordance with the Copyright, Designs and Patents Act 1988.

All rights reserved.

No part of this publication may be reproduced, stored in a retrieval system, or transmitted, in any form or by any means, electronic, mechanical, photocopying, recording or otherwise, without the prior permission of the copyright owners.

ISBN 978-1-910779-15-6 (Paperback)

Published by

Oxford eBooks

Dedicated to my wife.
Debra Georgina Pritchard 1960-2020

*My love.*
*Our passion.*
*You are genuine and true.*
*Were the words I used.*
*Before making love to you.*

*Three years have passed.*
*Without you by my side.*
*Giving each other.*
*Hugs and kisses then a bit on the side.*

*Thirty six years of wedded bliss.*
*Awakened each morning Debra.*
*Feeling your sensuous kiss.*

*Composing our poems.*
*Shall forever remain.*
*Then off to bed.*
*We are at it again.*

Rest in peace Debra.
Love Poet Andrew x

# Contents

| | | |
|---|---|---|
| 1. | Not loneliness but laughter | 7 |
| 2. | Popular Oxford haircuts | 10 |
| 3. | Vaccine call-up – but which one? | 12 |
| 4. | Truth Drug for Dominic Cummings | 14 |
| 5. | Dodgy Downing Street garden Party | 16 |
| 6. | Vaccine nightmare from outer space | 20 |
| 7. | The tsunami wave | 22 |
| 8. | A Bug's Life | 24 |
| 9. | Being Sozzled is Plan B | 28 |
| 10. | Steer Sir Keir to the Beer | 30 |
| 11. | World leaders become lab rats | 32 |
| 12. | Truffle-Truss vs Six-Pack Sunak | 34 |
| 13. | War decided by ice hockey match | 36 |
| 14. | Queen Elizabeth and her motley crew | 38 |
| 15. | Gentleman Gareth Southgate, a Winner | 40 |
| 16. | The Tattoo | 44 |
| 17. | Halloween Nightmare | 46 |
| 18. | Bus tour experience through the portal | 48 |

# Not loneliness but laughter

Loneliness is a punishment of time.

Your life sentence, having committed no crime.

Emailing church service, time and date.

Smart dress code, attending this wake.

Unlimited champagne, food on platters, just been baked.

Not Kipling cakes, slices of pizza served on cardboard plates.

In-laws arrive, they're never late, for free food and drink, mementos to take.

"Please help yourself, as a keepsake."

There's the sisters, all had affairs, more kids to feed than steps on flight of stairs.

That's her brother coughing up the drive,
   smoking forty a day, looking barely alive.

"I like dragging on Capstan King-Size."

"Stub it out, before you go inside."

Portmanteaus in hand,

"Ready, steady, go!"

Squabbling like cats, screeching out,
   hearing echo.

Grabbing this, breaking that.

"Deb promised me her Royal Ascot hat."

Bringing on premature panic attack.

Youngest sibling, spoilt brat,

"I want that!"

Causing suspected heart attack.

Richer Pickings, first bedroom, top of the
   stairs.

Breaking banister,

"We don't sodding care!"

"I'm the eldest, Rembrant is mine!"

"Otherwise shall snap your spine!"

Brother wheezing in behind,

"Lost me ciggies, but never mind."

Suddenly awaken, from self-induced sleep. Seven days, that's a week.

Viewing *Under the hammer*,

"That piece belonged to my Deb!"

Switched off telly, turned on laptop instead.

To my astonishment and dismay,

Items not sold, appear on ebay.

# Popular Oxford haircuts

Entering barbers, with my great mullet of tea cosy hair.

Sat down tentatively, in reclining chair.

Buzz-cut from left to right giving your scalp plenty of sunlight, sounds extreme.

Hang on a mo...

What are my options? Please let me know.

The ***mohawk*** would suit you through and through.

Just left the reservation to visit you.

Cut ***zero one two***, no sheep shearing practice on my head for you.

What about, three-two-one?

Reminiscing on that late eighties game show he once appeared on.

***Ceasar*** grand cut, did nothing for him.

Though it fed my cat.

Scraps went in Dusty Bin.

***Taper and fade***, getting really frustrated at this stage.

Recommend the ***pompadour***.

Dropped my money, then ran out the door.

# Vaccine call-up – but which one?

My smartphone shone bright, what message could this be?

COVID innoculation at ten-past-three.

Petrified of having needle injected in me, downed a stiff drink immediately.

Entering surgery at allotted time, sweating profusely from my neck to my back, then down to my spine.

Squarkbox on wall Tannoyed me: "Nurse will administer AZ vaccine in room three."

"Remove your mask! Speak up man!"

"That Panda Pee vaccine's not going in my arm!"

"Have you been drinking sir?"

"Sorry, but yes."

She sent me next door for Pfizer instead!

# Truth Drug for Dominic Cummings

Scopolamine was legally prescribed.

Loosening the tongue of Dominic Cummings, thorn in prime minster's side.

Known as 'Dom' for Pérignon Champagne he frequently indulged upon, standing up before panel elite looking drowsy on his feet.

"You visited Barnard Castle, who did you meet?"

Christian was his name, renowned open heart surgeon with familiar last name.

Extracted iffy-dicky-dodgy-ticker for a replicated pace-maker heart.

Spotted by police who were making sand castles on their local beach.

"Lockdown rule doesn't apply to you."

Sped back from Durham to London without missing a beat.

# Dodgy Downing Street garden Party

COBRA cabinet meeting just finished on first floor.

More venom in snake-bite throwing his darts on TV next door.

Prime Minister looking very perplexed and forlorn, watching Carrie cuddle baby Romy on Downing Street lawn.

"Is that ten or eleven I've conceived to be born?"

Recognising Matt Hancock facing other way over there, trying his best to get a suntan on bald-patch head of hair.

Suave, sophisticated Rees-Mogg arrives in his own inevitable way.

His cream cracker's well suited for the lawn terrace top table today.

Dominic Cummings arrives by tandem with eye specialist on back, checking his vision so he can ride back.

Can only surmise the dirty rat that took a garden photo from top of PM's luxury Downing Street flat.

As I am dreaming "Let the litigation begin, to have an ending we must start at the beginning."

Crafty, cunning Champagne Dom, warp-speeding from Durham to London to position zoom lens camera with remote control on.

"Cheese everyone!"

Photo is taken, now I'm long gone.

# Vaccine nightmare from outer space

Creatures so scary, monsters took flight.

I was administered AZ vaccine last night.

Vivid, dark dreams were messaging thee.

The Ouija board, directed me.

"Take Pfizer vaccine in your neck and your knee."

Quickly realising what AZ could mean, Another Zombie appears on the wide screen.

Outer space warning, signaled by ray of light, "AZ vaccine affects your longevity each night."

Throbbing head, aching neck, was preventing my ability to get out of bed.

Jesus! What do I do?

So I took Moderna vaccine to combat the other two.

Hoping this nightmare dream will never happen again, I'm making damn sure this poem will end.

# The tsunami wave

I opened my window to the smell of the sea.

Then took in a lungful of "What the hell out there in the distance is that, way out at sea?"

A large tsunami wave, was heading for me.

These waves were huge, a surfer's delight.

I was sweating like crazy, not a pleasant sight.

Glued to the floor, bewildered what to do.

I grabbed my cat and my dog came too.

Like a gazelle, I leapt to the floor, and warned others to hide, and shut their back door.

But did these lovely people believe me?

Did they heck!

They ran to the nearest boozer for a swift pint instead.

# A Bug's Life

The Natural History Museum, along with Oxford Age UK,

Have organised a bug hunting tour in Radley Marshes today.

There is Stephen, Tech Buddy Age UK, in the reeds at Radley Lake on this sunny day.

With 'Quack-Quack' whistle, wearing camouflage hat, stalking isolated mallard with camera social distancing from pack.

We see duck a-la-orange, vacuum packed, while young man Adam displays his first container bug.

Entomologist Hayley calls out, "Is this the only Hornet about?" as one person pulls his comic out.

Darren whispers quickly, "You must watch this."

We all gather tightly knit, watching docile wasp settle on a wild carrot, slowly evolving into Jasper Carrot.

Back at the office, digesting scrumptious scones and cream teas, Louis tries desperately to educate me.

"What is the difference between flies and bees?"

"One has a zipper, the other stings my knee!"


Like London has its Rotherhithe, we have dung beetles, Nags Head, Hythe Bridge Street, Oxford Westside.

This is their story, some lived, most died, only four ever reached manhood.

This is your Bug's Life on how they survived.

Nags Head coaching Inn was the place to be seen.

Rolling dung balls, where horses had been.

Eating foetus droppings, they all tucked in.

With free dung balls on tap, long queues formed to take a nap.

Civil war breaks out.

Pesticide chemical attack.

Panic sets in.

Colonies of dung beetles cease existing.

Four quick thinking beetles burrow underground.

Surviving on dung beetle balls they came across in lost and found.

Focusing minds, occupying their time, they form a band with whatever instruments they could find.

Returning to surface, "Where do we go?"

Crawling to visit the most wealthiest beetle they know.

Sadly arriving, they say a prayer, then drive his VW Beetle away from there.


Evolution, this poem is all about, now into adulthood, their names are banded about.

Fans using clap nets give spontaneous applause.

To Ringo, John, George and Paul.

# Being Sozzled is Plan B

Bottles of booze is prime minister's Plan B.

For every employee, arriving at three, must carry a gladstone, filled with burgundy, beaujolais, biscuits and brie.

It's a wino's delight.

Paralytic partying throughout Downing Street every Friday night.

With party swinging now in full flow, there's baby Wilf's swing, let's give it a go.

Scrambling to sit on best part of seat, undercarriage problems between left and right feet.

This unisex ride, rising way up high.

She's on top perched on bare thigh, screaming "Let's reenact *Reach for the sky.*"

Spotted, gasping for air from search lights below, descending very quickly, Oxygen low.

Inflating barrage balloons she possesses up top.

Grasping his rudder to slow this ride down.

Swing, now broken they crash to the ground.

Standing up, both do stare.

"Let's be honest, we don't sodding care!"

# Steer Sir Keir to the Beer

Accusing Sir Keir of breaking lockdown rule two tier, summising reality begins:

This ex-prosecutor, don't hang her but shoot her was filmed drinking a bottle of beer.

Returning from cellar hauling crates of Angela's favourite Stella, Rayner decides to walk in.

Pouting lips, sensuous grin, face hair growing on delicate chin.

"Let's all gather to play this board game!"

On the floor, it's Twister again.

Spreading her legs, moving one arm.

"My turn next to spin for colour on card."

Crossing her legs, red over blue getting in practice for PM Qs.

Tory mole informed Durham police, detailed account of partying feast.

Not mud slinging, but mud singing!

Rhyming in tune to the beat, both jump up dancing to *Tiger Feet*.

Questioned by police on what took place,

Sir Keir Starmer, you smell of malt and hops! You're a bloody disgrace!

# World leaders become lab rats

The hierarchy gather, world leaders in room four, straight or bent no matter.

Coronavirus affects us all.

Different vaccines need to be tried then applied, allowing mankind to survive.

Emmanuel Macron raises his right arm, dreaming of those alphabet women he once managed to charm.

Angela Merkel raises her arm – this is not Sieg Heil, Ma'am.

Moderna, Moderna I feel no pain, hoping to stay in office for another term again.

Boris raises both arms.

Johnson & Johnson for me, developed by my brother, my sister and my future wife-to-be.

Never shy, he decides to brag, "This vaccine was concocted in baby Wilfred's bath tub."

For once in my lifetime, presidents Putin and Biden shake hands and wholeheartedly agree.

Until sleepy Joe stumbles, injecting Sputnik into Vladimir's knee.

# Truffle-Truss vs Six-Pack Sunak

Truss verses Sunak face to face.

Stupendous, audatious prime-time television debate.

Liz creates economic almighty fuss, recruiting more pen-pushing jobs for the fuzz.

Lay it on thick, Richie Sunak, spreading his wealth like tubs of Lurpak.

Representing Richmond as conservative constituency MP.

First four letters RICH describe me.

Grinning Richie six-pack Sunak, "My plan is tax. Police on the beat, less money to keep, desitute and homeless, but not Prada shoes on my feet."

This proud British Indian ex-chancellor, looking for larger premises if becoming prime minister.

"My reservation shall be Chequers, with wife, children and whole of Delhi!"

Liz interrupts, "Let me speak!"

"My solution, removing congestion traffic from motorway, for cattle-trucks of migrants leaving England today."

"Incentive: Free breakfast, lunch, roast dinner, orange and tea."

"Destination Rwanda, arriving as supper, country is very hungry!"

# War decided by ice hockey match

Ukraine your neck to get the best view.

Watching satellite television along with all Russians like you.

This ***ice hockey*** match deciding this land is mine or I want more.

No lives lost,

Just blood, cuts and bruises galore.

Procrastinating leaders ***face off*** in presidential palace on ***ice sheet*** floor.

Renowned president Putin delivering one-liners like:

"Flush your lav Vlod"

to opposition entourage
   coming through door.

Giving him that ***icing*** stare, actor, comic,
   director too:

"I am President Zelensky
   Who the bloody hell are you?!"

Catching a mouthful of ***puck*** –

"You incompetent comedian cretin!"

Putin is boot in his delicate disputed
   Donbas region...

Followed by a converted Nippon he had
   not foreseen,

bringing this match to a ***frosty*** ending.

# Queen Elizabeth and her motley crew

1947, it all began.

Prince Phillip flexed his big-end in series one Land Rover he designed some specifications on.

Prince Charles was first, loves to dance, with Diana, Camilla too.

Watch out Sophie, you're next on the floor,

He's got his eye on you.

In stark contrast, let's not forget, Falkland helicopter pilot Prince Andrew of guts and grace.

Saved many a life diverting exocet missiles to a much safer place.

Returning home, he sought out Koo, giving her his medal, and photo of chopper he flew.

Addicted to horses, like her grandma and mum, riding her rocking horse Daddy shouts out,

"What's its name, Anne?"

"Doublet, I've won!"

Like his Action Man toy hero, Prince Edward longed becoming a royal marine.

Instead became really useful at stage production, using aquamarine in the opening scene.

Your majesty, the secret is now out.

Remarkable longevity, to a wonderful life.

Elixier on jam sandwiches Ma'am.

Accompanied by Paddington bear at platinum Jubilee concert night.

# Gentleman Gareth Southgate, a Winner

Remembering a time last century ago, world cup '66 leather footballs, wages were low.

Fifty five years ago, I was just a nipper – string vest on my back, holes in me slipper.

A crescendo of noise bellows out from the stands, believing football is coming home to England.

Has Gareth got any more tricks up his sleeve? Here's one we did not foresee.

Tannoy announces late team sheet change, Gareth Southgate is playing again!

Three lions blazoned across his chest, leads young cubs out to face Italy.

Euro final, the acid test.

Deadlock deep into added time, what's Gareth got on his mind?

Tracksuit comes off, crowds chant his name, "Hurry up, get yourself on, before whistle is blown to end this game."

Southgate gets off the bench with only seconds to go of extra time to play.

Penalty shoot-out will decide this game today.

At England fans' end, Gareth places the ball.

"They'll bloody lynch me if I miss from the spot like I did before!"

"What's this monstrosity facing me? Goalkeeper like leaning tower of Pisa without toppings pepperoni."

Shimmy to the right, connect with the
 left, ball goes in – back of the net, ending
 twenty five years of excruciating pain.
 I will never kick another football ever
 again.

# The Tattoo

While you dream in your self-induced emancipated sleep,

A tattoo on your blank canvas chest would look very sweet.

Soft toned inks reflecting colours of the rainbow.

Using precision sharpened needle from work bench below,

Your subscription is paid as I work rather slow.

Give me the signal.

Green indicates go.

But where else on your anatomy would you like more tatts on show?

On both arms, around the neck, matching inside left or right leg.

Itchy on back, canoodling in bed.

The one place a tattoo can never go.

On your foot, matching amputated big toe.

# Halloween Nightmare

Hallucinating dreams, engulfing torture and pain. Halloween night returns to haunt us again.

Brace yourself for:
decapitation, debauchery, despicable, delirious, delectable, delight.

Freddie's back!

It's one minute past midnight, different monsters appear on the scene:

Frankenstein meets cyclops.

He has a bolt, the other glass eye.

They try pulling Herman Munster, as he walks on by.

Spotting Dracula with female quest, struggling to quell his bloodthirsty zest.

Jumping her bones in coffin below, she starts crypt kicking from fangs left in neck.

Blood sucking vampire devours milk churn-knockers instead.

Then wings it to castle for fresh gnasher set.

# Bus tour experience through the portal

My cheerful, charming, curvaceous Maggie.

While reciting a poem, to you on city sightseeing oxford tour bus, upper deck, front seat,

What happened next, is just a blur.

Describing my story as it did occur.

Travelling at pace down St Margaret's Road formally known as Gallows-Baulk Road.

Disintegrated body parts resurface from potholes ahead.

Bus driver stomps on the brakes, for shuddering bone crunching stop.

Jolly Jack transcends into epileptic shock.

On the floor in a giant heap, tourists shout loud "What the hell happened"

As we rise to our feet, driver bellows out, "Radcliffe Infirmary round the next bend!"

Jolly Jack decides to floor it again.

All arriving at emergency A&E.

Catching our breath, desperately requiring the lavatory.

E.C.G. Showing personal best.

Heart pumping ticker recording world's fastest time.

We reach for defibrillators in the nick of time.

# Acknowledgement to Author

Andrew George Pritchard.

Born 18 December 1955 from excellent stock.

I have always found poetry very Therapeutic and gratifying.

Using the spoken word, composing poems for these charities.

Thanking these organisations:

Age UK Oxfordshire, in particular Tech buddy Troy Bryan.

The Archway Foundation in Oxford, helping people battle Loneliness while supporting my poetry through their newsletter.

Presently workling for City Sightseeing Oxford performing on open top bus as tour guide Poet Andrew.

Finally, acknowledging Maggie for being very inspirational in formulatiung Title to this book.

## *Pied Poet Andrew of Oxford*

Join Poet Andrew on a walking tour of Oxford with poetry recitals on the city's famous alumni.

**www.piedpoetandrewofoxford.co.uk**

www.ingramcontent.com/pod-product-compliance
Lightning Source LLC
Chambersburg PA
CBHW041153110526
44590CB00027B/4214